Books in the Linkers series

Homes discovered through Art & Technology
Homes discovered through Geography
Homes discovered through History
Homes discovered through Science

Myself discovered through Art & Technology
Myself discovered through Geography
Myself discovered through History
Myself discovered through Science

Toys discovered through Art & Technology
Toys discovered through Geography
Toys discovered through History
Toys discovered through Science

Water discovered through Art & Technology
Water discovered through Geography
Water discovered through History
Water discovered through Science

Food discovered through Art & Technology
Food discovered through Geography
Food discovered through History
Food discovered through Science

Journeys discovered through Art & Technology
Journeys discovered through Geography
Journeys discovered through History
Journeys discovered through Science

First published 1997 A&C Black (Publishers) Limited
35 Bedford Row, London WC1R 4JH

ISBN 0-7136-4763-9

A CIP catalogue record for this book is available from the British Library.
Copyright © 1997 BryantMole Books

Commissioned photographs by Zul Mukhida

Design by Jean Wheeler

Acknowledgements

Cephas; 14 (left), Chapel Studios; Zul Mukhida 16 (left), Bruce Coleman; Andy Purcell (cover), 7 (left), Janos Jurka 11 (right), James Davis; 6, 10, Eye Ubiquitous; Michael Reed 11 (left), L. Fordyce 13 (right), Paul Seheult 20 (right), Steve Lindridge 21, Positive Images; 7 (right), Tony Stone Images; Matthew McVay 3 (left), Tony Craddock 5 (left), David Frazier 5 (right), Howard Grey 8, Annette Soumillard 9 (top), Andy Sacks 12, 14 (right), Mark Segal 17, Zefa; 2, 3 (right), 13 (left), 15, 16 (right), 20 (left), 22

Printed and bound in Italy by L.E.G.O.

Food

discovered through
Geography

Karen Bryant-Mole

Contents

A & C Black • London

Food

We all eat food every day.
But where does it come from
and how does it get to us?

Farms
Most of the food we eat is
grown or produced on farms.
There are many different types
of farm.
This is a farm where vegetables
are grown.

Shops
From the farm, the food might be taken to a market or to a factory.
Eventually, most food ends up in shops, where we can buy it.

People
The business of producing food is called the food industry. There are lots of people involved in the food industry. They include farmers, shop assistants, lorry drivers and factory workers.

This book will help you to find out more about food and how it reaches your home.

3

Cereals

Any food that is grown can be called a crop. Some of the most important crops grown on farms are cereals.

Grasses
Cereals are special grasses, with seeds that can be eaten. They include wheat, oats and barley. They are made into things like flour and breakfast cereals. Cereals are also used as food for animals.

wheat

oats

barley

Farmers
Farmers on cereal farms have many different jobs to do.
Their work includes ploughing fields, sowing seeds,
caring for the young seedlings and cutting, or
harvesting, the crops.

Weather
The weather is very important to cereal farmers.
Seeds need rain to start growing but too much rain
would wash the seeds away.
Crops need sunshine to ripen.
Wind and rain could flatten the crops and ruin them.

Animals

Some farmers keep animals.

Meat
Animals are often kept for meat.
The most usual animals to keep for meat are pigs, cows and sheep.
Some farms have rather more unusual animals, like this ostrich!

Dairy farms

Farms where cows are kept for their milk are called dairy farms.
The cow below is being milked by a machine in a special building called a milking parlour.

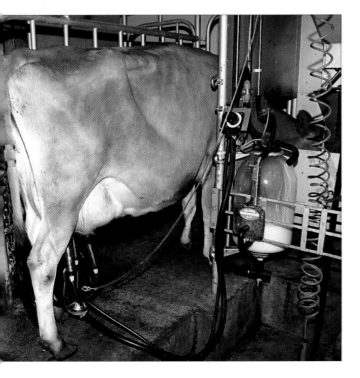

Buildings

There are many types of buildings on farms.
There is usually a farmhouse, where the farmer and his family live.
There may be buildings that are used as homes for animals.
The barn in the picture above is used to store hay for the animals to eat and straw for their bedding.

7

Fruit and vegetables

Fruit and vegetables are grown on farms that are sometimes called market gardens.

Fruit

There are two different sorts of fruit; soft fruit and tree fruit. Tree fruit includes fruit such as apples and pears.
A piece of land where fruit trees grow, is called an orchard.
Soft fruit includes fruit like gooseberries, raspberries and strawberries.
Soft fruit usually grows on bushes or low-growing plants.

Vegetables

Vegetables are plants that can be eaten.

Some vegetables are grown outdoors in fields.

Others, like these lettuces, are grown in glass houses, where they are kept warm and are sheltered from wind and rain.

Seasons

Different fruit and vegetables are harvested at different times of the year.

Blackberries and pears are autumn fruits.

French beans and radishes are ready for picking during the summer.

Why not find out when other fruit and vegetables are harvested?

Land

The sort of food that farmers produce, often depends on the type of soil they have on their farm.

Arable land
Land that can be used to grow crops is known as arable land.
Crops need a good, rich soil in which to grow.

Pasture land

Grass will grow in soil that is too poor for crops.

Cows and other animals eat grass.

Land where grass grows well and which is used by animals for grazing is called pasture land.

Hills

It is even possible to farm land with very poor soil.

These sheep live on rocky hillsides.

There is less grass than on good pasture land but the sheep can still find enough to eat.

11

Climate

The type of weather in an area is known as its climate. Around the world there are many types of climate. Different types of food grow in different climates.

Britain
In Britain we have warm summers and cold, wet winters. These are good conditions for growing fruit such as apples, and vegetables like potatoes and sprouts.

Hot summers, cool winters

Some countries, like Greece and Italy, have hot, dry summers and cool, but not cold, winters. Oranges, grapes, olives and peaches grow well in places like this.

Hot and wet

Some places, such as India and parts of China, are hot and wet all year round.
Rice is a popular crop to grow in these areas. It is the main food of the people who live there.

You could find out about other foods and the type of climate they prefer.

13

Seas and rivers

There is food in our seas and rivers too.

Rivers
The water in rivers and lakes is called fresh water.
Fish such as salmon and trout live in fresh water. Freshwater fish are often caught using a rod and line.

Seas
The water in the sea is salty. Saltwater fish, such as cod and plaice, are caught by fishermen using nets.
We can also eat other sea creatures, such as prawns, crabs and lobsters.

Fish farms

This is a special farm, called a fish farm.
The baby fish hatch out into a nursery tank.
As they grow, they are moved into different tanks or ponds.
It is easy to catch fish when you know where they are!

Selling

Once food has been grown or produced, it has to be sold.

Markets
Farmers often sell their produce at markets.
There are many different types of market. They include livestock markets, where animals are sold, fruit and vegetable markets and fish markets.

Export
Some of the food that farmers produce is sold to other countries. Anything that goes from our country to another country is called an export.
The wheat in the picture above will be exported to a country that does not grow enough wheat of its own.

16

Selling directly
Sometimes, farmers sell their produce directly to factories or supermarkets.
There are often strict rules about the food.
Supermarkets like the produce to be a certain size, colour and shape.

Factories

Much of our food goes to a factory before we eat it.

Packaging
Some foods go to a factory to be packaged. These potatoes have been weighed and put into a bag.

Preserving
Some foods go to a factory to be preserved. Preserving food makes it stay good to eat for a long time.

18

Canning and freezing are two ways of preserving food.

Recipes
Sometimes, food is sent to a factory to be mixed with other foods to make a particular dish.
Mashed potato has been piped over some fish in a sauce to make this Fisherman's Pie.

Buying food

Delivering food

When food is ready to be sold, it is taken to shops and supermarkets in lorries.
Food such as bread, fruit and vegetables are usually delivered early in the morning, so that they are really fresh.
Other foods such as cereals and bottled drinks can be delivered at any time of day.

Supermarkets

Many people buy their food from a supermarket.
In a supermarket it is possible to buy every type of food in the same place.

Shops
Some shops sell
particular types
of food.
A greengrocer sells
fruit and vegetables.
A baker sells bread,
cakes and biscuits.
This shop only
stocks cheese!

21

Around the world

The food in our shops does not only come from this country.

Imports
Buying food from other countries and bringing it into our country is called importing food.
These sacks of coffee are being imported from Brazil.

Canned food

Much of the food we import is preserved in cans.
The pineapple pieces in the picture below were canned in Thailand, where the pineapples were grown. The cans were sent to our country by boat.

Fresh food

Most supermarkets now sell fresh fruit and vegetables from countries all around the world.
Some foods, like these paw-paws, are imported by plane so that they will still be fresh when they reach our shops.

Why not look at the labels on the foods in your home and find out where they are from?

Glossary

bedding what animals sleep on
conditions how things are
directly straight, without going
  anywhere else first
grazing when animals eat grass
  growing in a field

industry a particular sort of work or
  business
livestock farm animals
packaged put into packets, bags,
  boxes, bottles or tins
ploughing turning over soil
sowing planting

Index

How to use this book

Each book in this series takes a familiar topic or theme and focuses on one area of the curriculum: science, art and technology, geography or history. The books are intended as starting points, illustrating some of the many different angles from which a topic can be studied. They should act as springboards for further investigation, activity or information seeking.

History
changes have taken place during the past one hundred years, relating to:
- the way food is produced
- how food is transported
- where and how food is bought
- the variety of food available
- the utensils used to prepare food
- how food is cooked
- where food is stored
- how food is preserved
- eating meals

FOOD
key concepts and activities explored within each book

Art and Technology
- food is prepared to make it taste good and look attractive
- chefs are creative with food
- some tools are especially designed for food
- food features in 'still life' works of art
- make a pizza
- design a menu
- print with food
- model a meal
- create a summer drink
- make a still life picture

Science
- all living things need food
- plants make their own food
- foods can be classified into different groups
- we need to eat a variety of foods
- our bodies use different types of food in different ways
- a healthy diet is important
- food travels through our digestive system
- smelling and tasting food involves our senses
- food changes when it is cooked or heated

Geography
- food is usually produced on farms
- there are different types of farm, where different types of food are produced
- climate and land-type determine the food produced
- food can be found in salt water and fresh water
- many foods are processed and packaged in factories
- food is sold in markets, supermarkets and shops
- food can be imported and exported